Being a Scientist

drip

splash

plop

Young learners need to know that scientists are not just workers wearing white jackets in laboratories. We do science when we

- cook breakfast
- mix paints to make new colors
- plant seeds in the garden
- watch a squirrel in a tree
- mark how tall we are on a growth chart, or
- look outside to see what the weather is like

The activities in this book relate to the National Science Education Standards (Science as Inquiry). When you follow the step-by-step lessons, your students will be doing science. They will

- observe
- predict
- compare
- order
- categorize

- ask meaningful questions
- conduct investigations
- record information
- communicate investigations and explanations
- use tools and equipment

What makes this book easy for you?

- The step-by-step activities are easy to understand and include illustrations where it's important.
- The resources you need are at your fingertips: record sheets; logbook sheets; and other reproducibles such as minibooks, task cards, and picture cards.
- Each science concept is presented in a self-contained section. You can decide to do the entire book or pick only those sections that enhance your own curriculum.

minibooks

task cards

logbooks

picture cards

Using Logbooks as Learning Tools

ScienceWorks for Kids emphasizes the use of logbooks to help students summarize and solidify learning.

Logbooks are valuable learning tools for several reasons:

• Logbooks give students an opportunity to put what they are learning into their own words.

• Putting ideas into words is an important step in internalizing new information. Whether spoken or written, this experience allows students to synthesize their thinking.

• Explaining and describing experiences helps students make connections between several concepts and ideas.

• Logbook entries allow the teacher to catch misunderstandings right away and then reteach.

• Logbooks are a useful reference for students and a record of what has been learned.

Two Types of Logbooks

This picture stands for class logbook

Throughout the unit, a class logbook will be used to record student understanding.

• Use large sheets of chart paper.

• Hold the pages together with metal rings.

Even though your students may not be reading, the responses can be read to them as a means of confirming and reviewing learning.

This picture stands for student logbook

Students process their understanding of investigations by writing or drawing their responses in individual student logbooks. Following the investigations are record and activity sheets that can be added to each student's logbook.

At the conclusion of the unit, reproduce a copy of the logbook cover on page 3 for each student. Students organize their pages and staple them with the cover.

page 3

Weather

Logbook

drip

splash

plop

Wind blowing!

Name:

Teacher Preparation

Weather Observation

Before beginning this unit on weather, purchase and/or prepare items to use in a weather station.

- outdoor thermometer (select one with large numbers for easier reading)
- rain gauge (again, select one with large numbers)
- wind vane (purchase a wind vane or make one following the diagram below)
- anemometer (purchase an anemometer or make one following the diagram below)

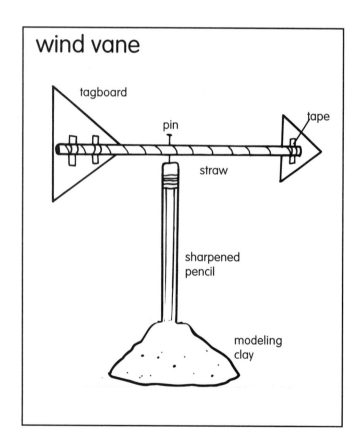

wind vane

tagboard

pin

tape

straw

sharpened pencil

modeling clay

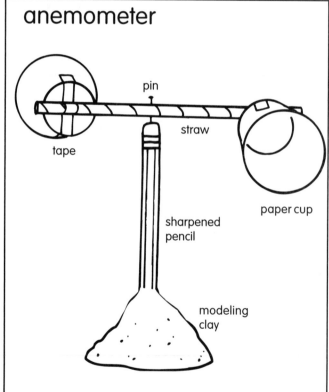

anemometer

pin

straw

tape

paper cup

sharpened pencil

modeling clay

A Weather Library

Take time to introduce students to your library of weather books. (See the inside back cover for the bibliography of nonfiction titles.)

 Learning About Weather • EMC 870

There are many kinds of weather.

Many Kinds of Weather

- Introduce the subject of weather by asking students to name and describe today's weather. Then have students name different kinds of weather. You may need to ask questions to help students verbalize what they know.

- Record student responses on a chart entitled "Weather." This chart will become the first page of the class weather logbook. Don't attempt to fill in information not offered by students. Return to the chart often to add more details as your students acquire more information.

Wind blowing!

Snow falling!

Weather

The sun is shining.

It is hot.

A little wind is blowing.

- Read *I Call It Sky* by Will C. Howell and/or appropriate sections from *Weather* by Pamela Chanko and Daniel Moreton or *Weather Everywhere* by Denise Casey. Ask students to recall the words for weather phenomena. Add weather words to the "Weather" chart.

Then have students act out movements for some of the different types of weather they named.

Name the Weather

- Show the cards on pages 9–12 to students one at a time. Ask students to describe what they see and to name the kind of weather.

- Using page 13, students draw and label two kinds of weather. This will be the first page of the students' individual logbooks.

- Using copies of the pictures on pages 9–12, students make "My Little Weather Book" to take home. Students color and cut out the cards, and then staple the pages together between pieces of construction paper for a cover.

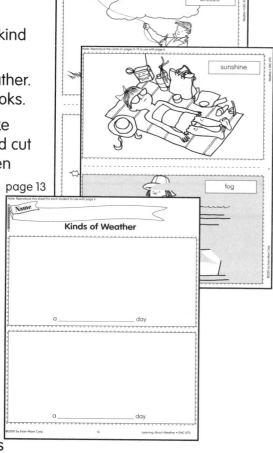

pages 9–12

page 13

What Should We Wear?

- Read *Warm Clothes* by Gail Saunders-Smith. Ask students to explain why the girls dressed as they did. Help students verbalize the idea that we dress to stay cool, warm, or dry depending on the kind of weather.

- Use the patterns on pages 14–16 to make pieces for a flannel or magnetic board. Place the child's figure on the flannel board. State a type of weather and ask students to decide what clothing the child would wear. Select students to place the clothing on the figure. Have students explain why the child would be wearing those pieces of clothing.

- Students name the kinds of things that can be done during specific types of weather (ride a sled on a snowy day; fly a kite on a windy day; splash in puddles on a rainy day).

  Using page 17, students fill in a type of weather, then draw a picture of themselves at play.

page 17

Learning About Weather • EMC 870

Rainy Weather

- Rain is one type of weather all students will have experienced. Have students share what they know about rain.

- Record student comments about rain on a chart entitled "Rain."

Rain

Drops of water fall out of the sky.

Rain comes from clouds.

drip

splash

plop

- Read *Listen to the Rain* by Bill Martin, Jr. and John Archambault, and then work with students to create a list of rain sounds (plop, splash, drip, etc.). Have each student select a word or phrase and illustrate it. Place the pictures in a cover to create a "Listen to the Rain" class book.

- Using page 18, students draw rain falling from the clouds onto an animal or a person.

- Ask students to think of why rain is important to plants, animals, and people. Add their responses to the "Rain" chart.

- Read and discuss the minibook on pages 19 and 20 to reinforce how important rain is to living things.

- Rainy Days—A Graph

  Use the raindrops on page 21 to make a yes/no graph. Students write their names on the raindrops, and then paste the drops in the correct column of the graph.

page 18

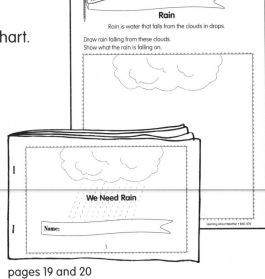

pages 19 and 20

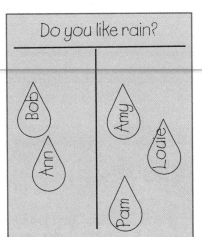

Do you like rain?

Bob

Ann

Amy

Louie

Pam

Snowy Weather

- Ask students to describe snow and to share their snow experiences.

- Record student comments about snow on a chart.

Snow

Snow is cold.

Snow is white.

Snow comes out of clouds in the sky.

- Read appropriate parts of *Snow Is Falling* by Franklyn M. Branley to help students understand what happens to create snow. Ask students to recall how snow is made. Make corrections or additions to the class logbook.

- Snowy Days—A Graph
  Use the snowflakes on page 22 to make a yes/no graph. Students write their names on the snowflakes, and then paste the flakes in the correct column of the graph.

- Using page 23, students draw a snow scene including flakes falling from the clouds.

- Discuss how snow can be fun (make snowmen; ride sleds) and how it can be a problem (very cold; blocks roads).

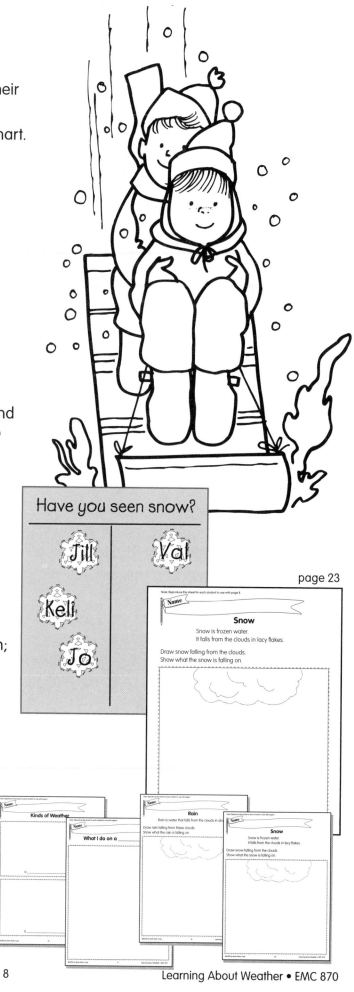

Have you seen snow?

Jill | Val

Keli

Jo

page 23

Name

Snow

Snow is frozen water.
It falls from the clouds in lacy flakes.

Draw snow falling from the clouds.
Show what the snow is falling on.

Logbook

Include these pages in each student's logbook.

Name

Kinds of Weather

Name

What I do on a

Name

Rain

Rain is water that falls from the clouds in dro

Draw rain falling from these clouds.
Show what the rain is falling on.

Name

Snow

Snow is frozen water.
It falls from the clouds in lacy flakes.

Draw snow falling from the clouds.
Show what the snow is falling on.

Weather • EMC 870

sunshine

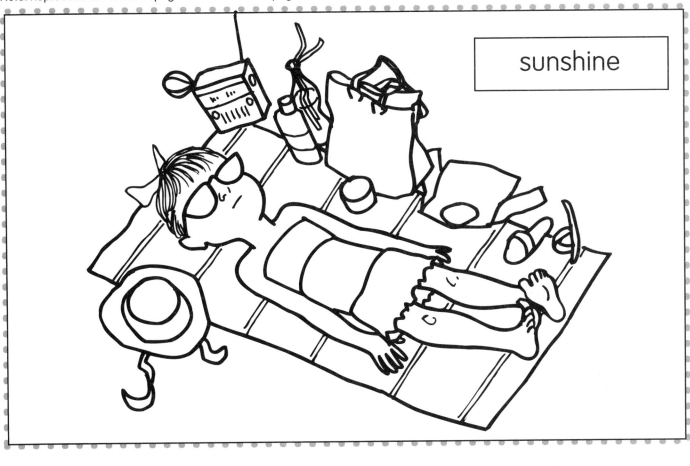

fog

rain

snow

clouds

hail

11

breeze

strong wind

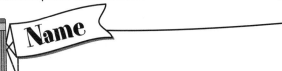

Kinds of Weather

a _____ day

a _____ day

Flannel Board Patterns

Learning About Weather • EMC 870

Clothing for Rainy and Sunny Days

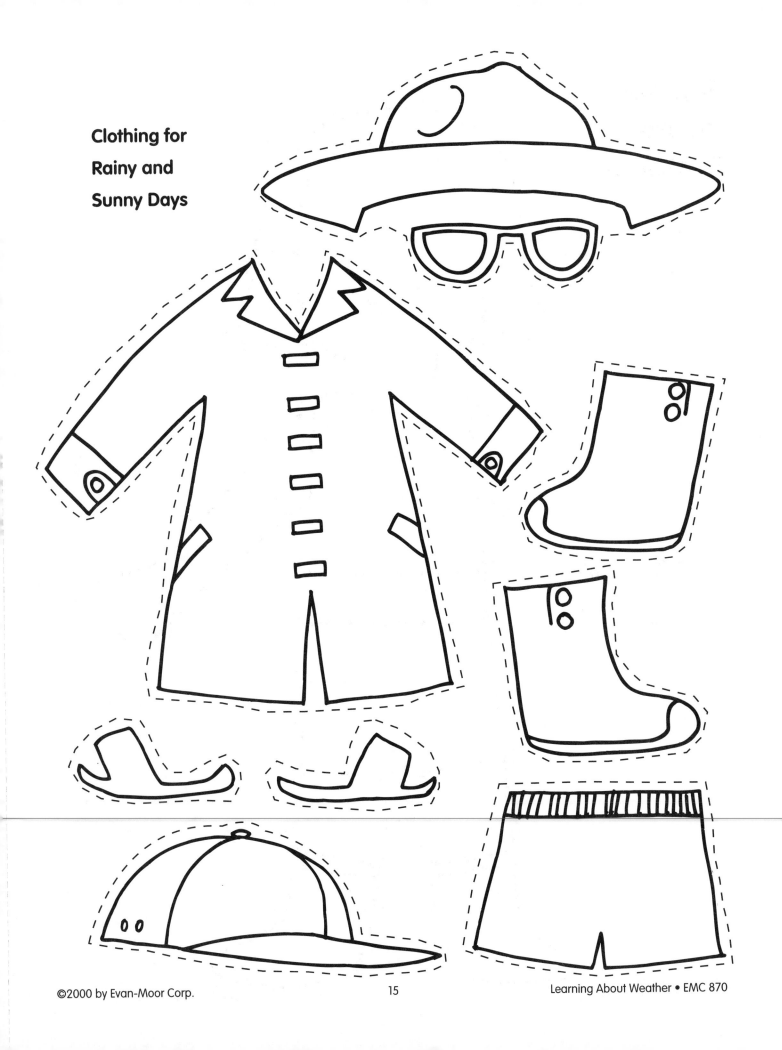

15

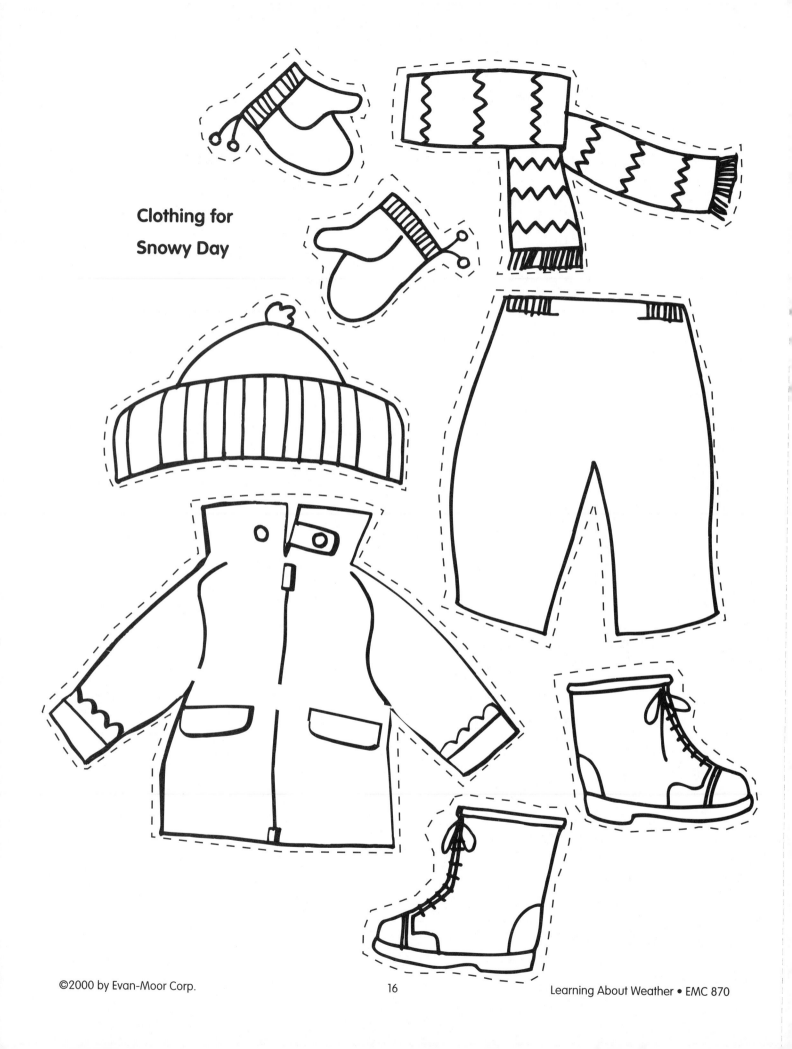

Clothing for Snowy Day

Learning About Weather • EMC 870

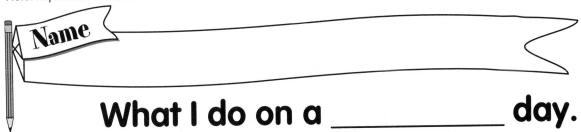

What I do on a _____ day.

Name

Rain

Rain is water that falls from the clouds in drops.

Draw rain falling from these clouds.
Show what the rain is falling on.

We Need Rain

Name:

1

Learning About Weather • EMC 870

Rain is water that falls from the sky.
Plants need the rainwater to live and grow.

2

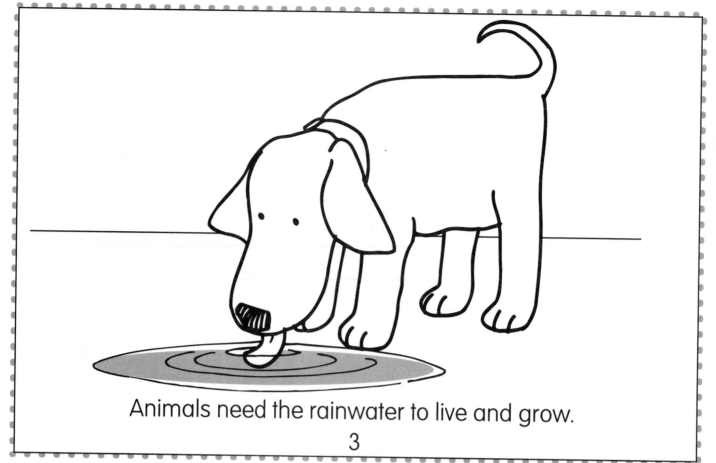

Animals need the rainwater to live and grow.

3

Learning About Weather • EMC 870

We need the rainwater to live and grow.

4

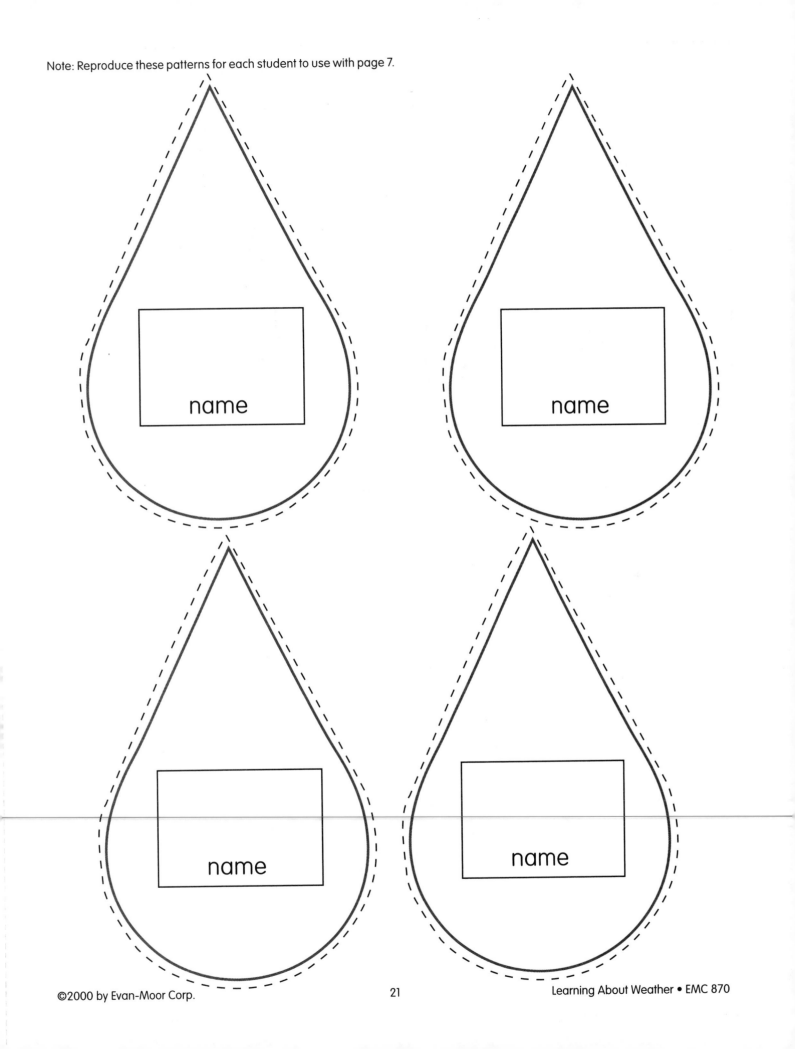

name

name

name

name

Name

Snow

Snow is frozen water.
It falls from the clouds in lacy flakes.

Draw snow falling from the clouds.
Show what the snow is falling on.

Weather changes from day to day.

Watching the Weather

- Review the kinds of words we use to describe weather (it's raining, the wind is blowing, it's foggy, the sun is shining, it's hot, etc.). Have students look out the classroom windows and describe the weather they see. Ask, "Is the weather different from what it was yesterday? How?"

- Read appropriate parts of *Weather Everywhere* by Denise Casey to expand students' understanding of weather changes.

- Using page 26, students are to draw a picture of the kind of weather they see outside. (Repeat this activity throughout the year, selecting specific types of weather to record.)

page 26

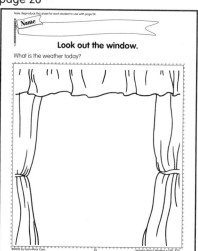

Weather Calendar

- Set up a weather calendar in your classroom. Using the weather symbols on page 27, have students pin the appropriate symbol(s) to the calendar each day. Change the symbols during the day if the weather makes a big change. At the end of the month, discuss the changes that have occurred.

page 27

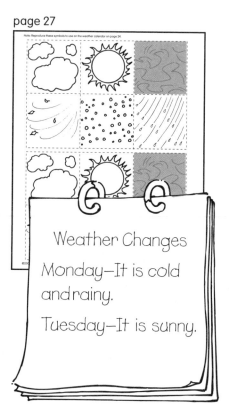

- After observing the changes in weather for several days, work with students to write a page for the class logbook.

Learning About Weather • EMC 870

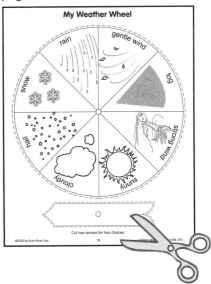

- If you have limited space on your daily calendar, make a weather wheel using the pattern on page 28. Paste it to a circle cut from tagboard or lightweight cardboard. Attach the arrows to the wheel with a large brass paper fastener. Move the arrows to the appropriate weather each day.

Making Connections

- Explain that changes in weather can affect plants. Ask students to describe changes they have seen in plants *(The leaves on our tree turned red. When it was hot my grandma's flowers looked droopy.)*

- Read the minibook on pages 29–32. Ask students to recall what happened to each plant when the weather changed.

- Record student responses on a chart as they describe what happens to plants when the weather changes.

pages 29–32

Plants Change

When it starts getting cold, leaves fall off some trees.

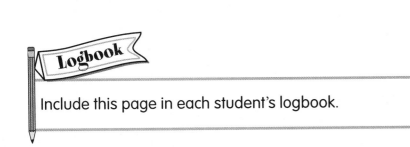

Logbook

Include this page in each student's logbook.

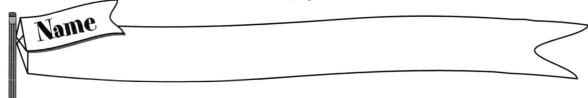

Name

Look out the window.

What is the weather today?

My Weather Wheel

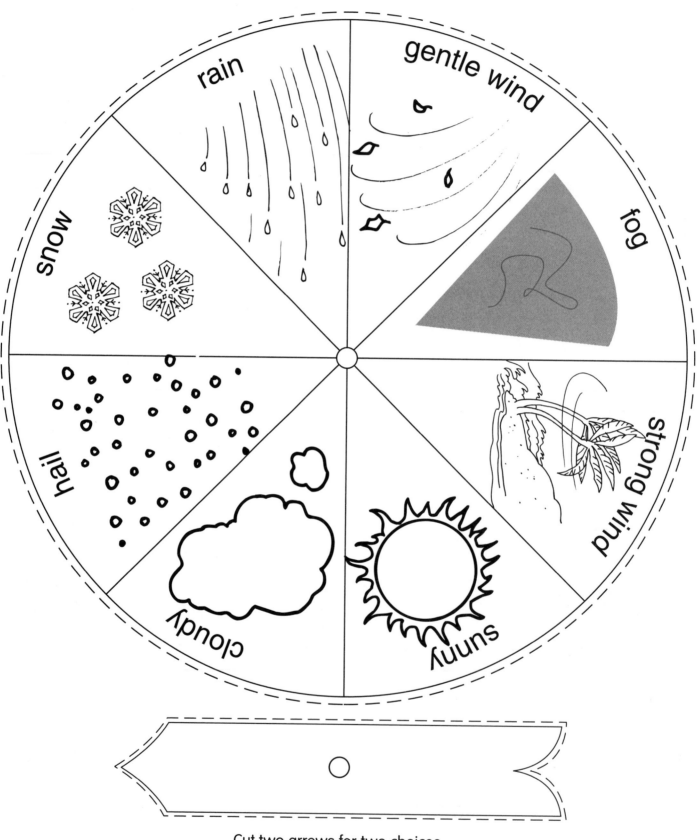

Cut two arrows for two choices.

28

Learning About Weather • EMC 870

Name:

When Weather Changes

1

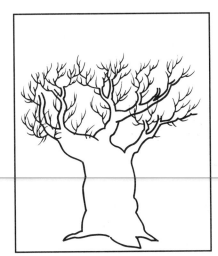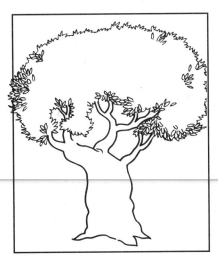

Plants change when the weather changes.

2

Here is a cactus in the hot, dry desert.

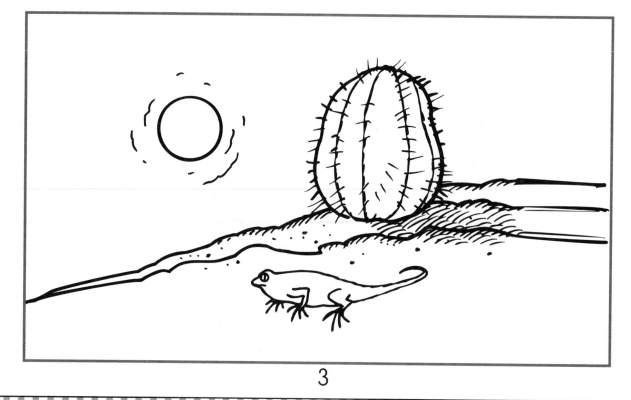

3

Learning About Weather • EMC 870

Here is the cactus after it has rained.

4

Here is a tulip on a cold winter day.

5

Learning About Weather • EMC 870

Here is the tulip on a warm spring day.

6

Here is a tree on a warm summer day.

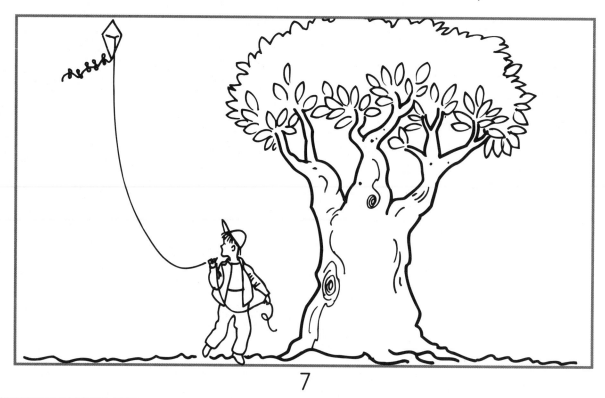

7

Learning About Weather • EMC 870

Here is the tree on a cool autumn day.

8

Weather changes from season to season.

Seasons Change

- Introduce seasonal weather changes by discussing what the weather is like at different times of the year where you live. Give the name for the current season. For example, say, "This time of year is called spring. It is one of the seasons of the year." Ask students to name other seasons they know. Use questioning to help if they have difficulty ("What do we call the time of year that is very cold?").

- As students name a season, ask them to describe it. Record their ideas on a chart.

- Read *Scamper's Year* by Jeff Kindley and/or books from the series *How Do You Know It's Summer?* (or *Winter, Fall, Spring*) by Allan Fowler. Ask students to recall what it is like during each season. Make additions or changes to the "Seasons" chart.

- Read the minibook on pages 35–37 with your students. Talk about what might be seen during each season. Ask, "Is this what summer (winter, spring, autumn) is like where we live? How is it the same? How is it different?"

- Have students complete the activity on pages 38 and 39. They are to cut out the pictures and paste them in boxes naming the correct seasons.

Seasons

Summer is hot.

We play outside.

Winter is cold.

Sometimes it snows.

pages 35–37

The Seasons

Summer,
Autumn,
Winter,
Spring,
This is what a year will bring.

Name:

1

©2000 by Evan-Moor Corp.

page 38

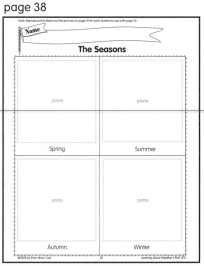

page 39

Seasons Wheel

- Using pages 40 and 41, students are to make a "seasons" wheel. Use the wheel to introduce the idea that seasons are weather changes that happen at the same time every year. Explain that things that happen over and over in a pattern are called *cycles*.

- Read appropriate parts of *Seasons* by Paul P. Sipiera and Diane M. Sipiera and *Sunshine Makes the Seasons* by Franklyn M. Branley.

- Have students think about what they've learned about the seasons. Ask them to name the season they like best and tell why. This can be done orally or as a drawing activity.

page 40

page 41

Making Connections

- Have students recall the ways they have seen animals or their behaviors change because of the weather. Explain that animals often have different behaviors during the different seasons.

- Share the picture cards on pages 42–45 one at a time. Discuss what each animal is doing. Let students decide what season of the year the picture illustrates.

- Record student responses about what happens to animals as the seasons change.

pages 42–45

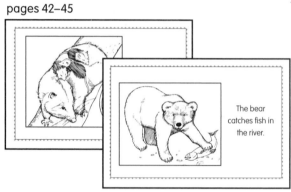

The bear catches fish in the river.

On TV I saw a bear go to sleep in a cave when it was cold.

page 46

How Do These Animals Change?

Match the animals.

Summer   Winter

- Using page 46, students match pictures of animals in the spring with pictures of the same animals in the winter.

Logbook

Include these pages in each student's logbook.

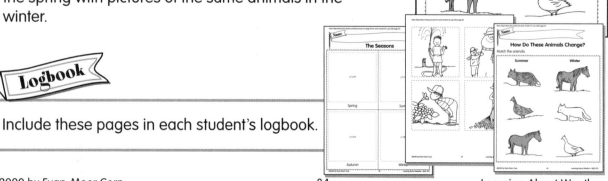

Summer

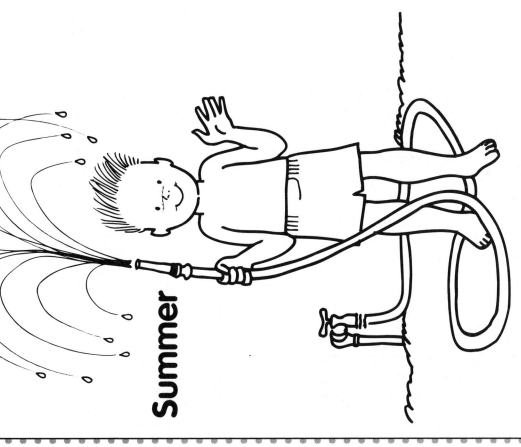

The days are long and warm.
In some places it is very hot.
How do you stay cool on a hot day?

2

The Seasons

Summer,
Autumn,
Winter,
Spring,
This is what a year will bring.

1

Name:

Autumn

Days are getting shorter. It is cooler, too. Some mornings there is frost.

Another name for autumn is "fall." Is this because leaves fall off the trees?

3

Winter

The days are much colder. Many parts of the earth are covered in snow.

Does it snow in the winter where you live?

4

Learning About Weather • EMC 870

©2000 by Evan-Moor Corp.

Spring

There may be more sunny days and it is a warmer.
Breezes blow and rain falls.

Do you see flowers blooming?

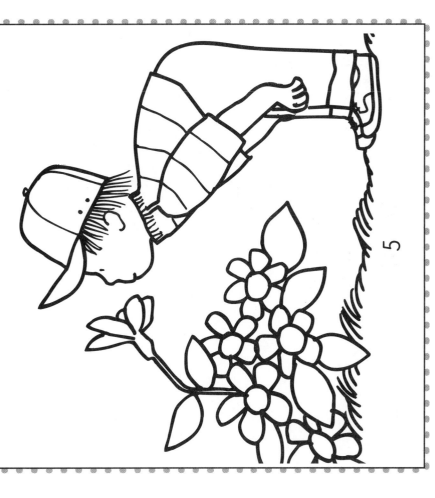

5

    Learning About Weather • EMC 870

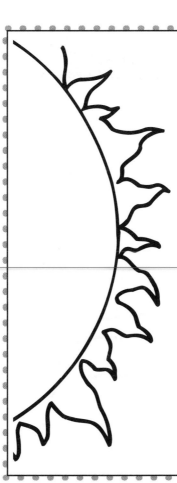

The seasons are not the same everywhere.

If you live where the sun shines most of the time, winter and summer may not be very different.

You might just have a rainy season and a dry season.

6

Name

The Seasons

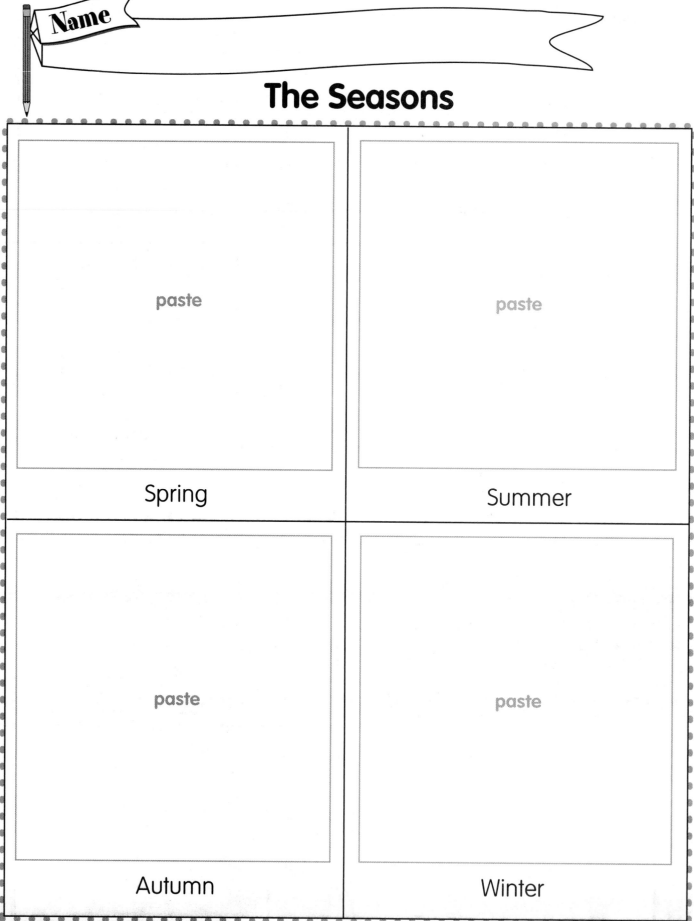

paste

paste

Spring

Summer

paste

paste

Autumn

Winter

Note: Reproduce these pictures for each student to use with page 38.

Learning About Weather • EMC 870

Seasons Wheel Pattern

Color.

Cut out.

Put together.

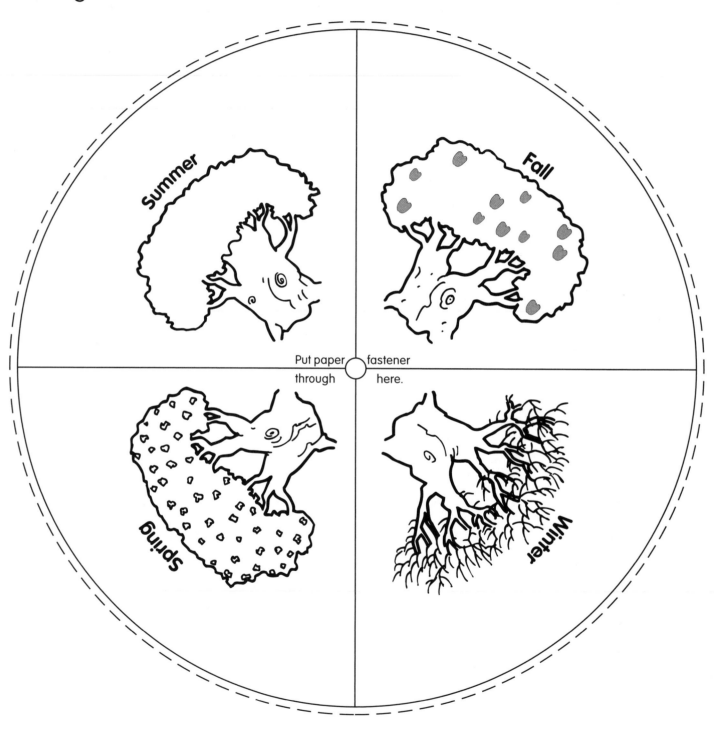

Summer

Fall

Put paper fastener
through here.

Spring

Winter

My Seasons Wheel

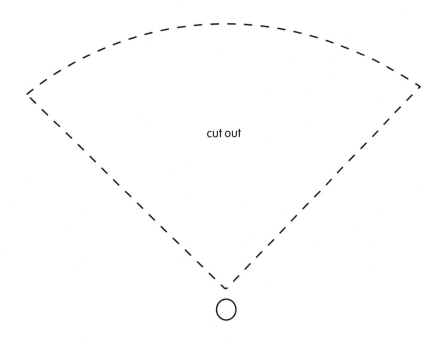

cut out

Turn the wheel to see the
cycle of the seasons.

Name:

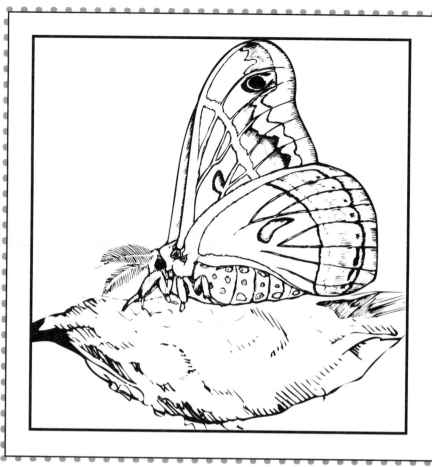

The moth hatches from a cocoon.

The geese migrate.

The opossum carries her babies on her back.

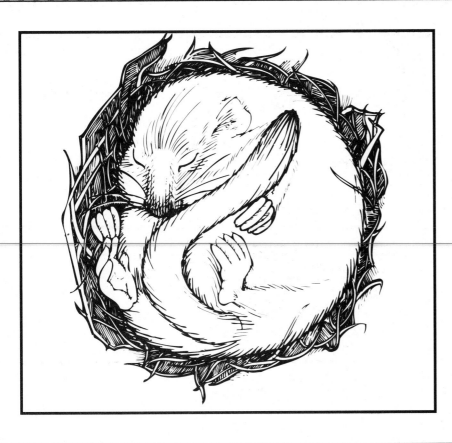

The dormouse hibernates.

The bear catches fish in the river.

The squirrel gathers nuts.

Hungry babies are in the nest.

The ptarmigan is as white as snow.

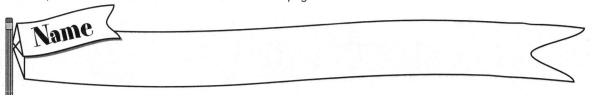

Name

How Do These Animals Change?

Match the animals.

Summer   Winter

       Learning About Weather • EMC 870

Temperature can be measured.

Measurement Tools

- Gather an assortment of measuring tools.

  1. Students identify the tools and tell what each would measure.

  2. Sort the tools by what they measure (time, length, weight, etc.).

  3. With student help, demonstrate how each tool is used.

- Ask students to describe a time when they were measured or when they measured something themselves.

- Read appropriate parts of *What Will the Weather Be?* by Lynda DeWitt to introduce students to how scientists measure weather. Explain to students that they will be using some tools that measure weather.

Making Connections

Ask students, "Have you ever seen a weather report on television?" Have students that have seen weather reports share what they heard and saw.

I saw a big map with numbers on it on TV.

A lady told us how hot it was.

Learning for Myself—We Can Measure Temperature

Show an outdoor thermometer. Explain to students that they will be using the thermometer to measure temperature. Conduct the investigation below.

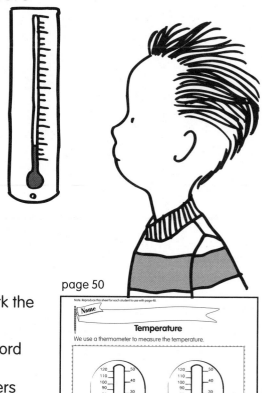

Materials

- outdoor thermometer
  (the largest one you can find)

- washable black marking pen

- record sheet on page 50,
  reproduced for each student

Steps to Follow

1. Place the thermometer where students can see it. Mark the thermometer to show the indoor temperature.

2. Have students mark the first thermometer on their record sheets by coloring up to the number. (You may need to mark the spot for students who cannot read numbers yet.) Ask students to predict what will happen to the thermometer when it is taken outside.

3. Take the thermometer outside. Wait 10 minutes and mark the temperature again. Observe what has happened.

4. Have students mark the temperature on the second thermometer on their record sheets.

5. Discuss what they observed ("Did the line go up or down? Does that mean it is warmer or colder outside?").

   - Place completed record sheets in students' logbooks.

   - Have students describe what they did to measure the temperature. Record their responses on a chart. Additions will be made to the chart as other aspects of weather are measured.

page 50

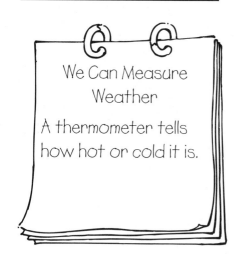

We Can Measure Weather

A thermometer tells how hot or cold it is.

Temperatures Change

Make a model of a thermometer using tagboard, red and white ribbon, a black marking pen, needle and thread, and a safety pin.

Materials

- 6" x 18" (15 x 45.5 cm) tagboard
- 18" (45.5 cm) red ribbon
- 18" (45.5 cm) white ribbon
- marking pen
- safety pin
- needle and thread
- Exacto® knife (adult use only)

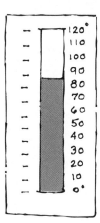

Steps to Follow

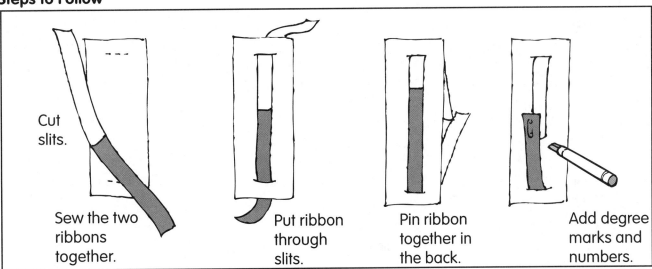

Cut slits.

Sew the two ribbons together.

Put ribbon through slits.

Pin ribbon together in the back.

Add degree marks and numbers.

Each day, read the temperature outdoors on a real thermometer. Select a student to move the ribbon up or down so the top of the red line marks the actual temperature. If your students cannot read the numbers yet, move the ribbon yourself and have students watch to see if it moves up or down. Then discuss whether the weather is hotter or colder than yesterday.

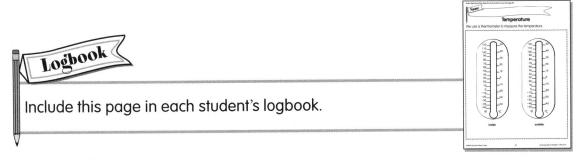

Logbook

Include this page in each student's logbook.

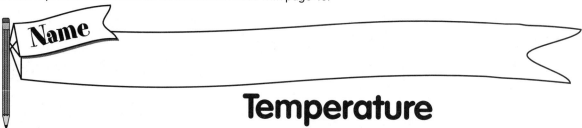

Temperature

We use a thermometer to measure the temperature.

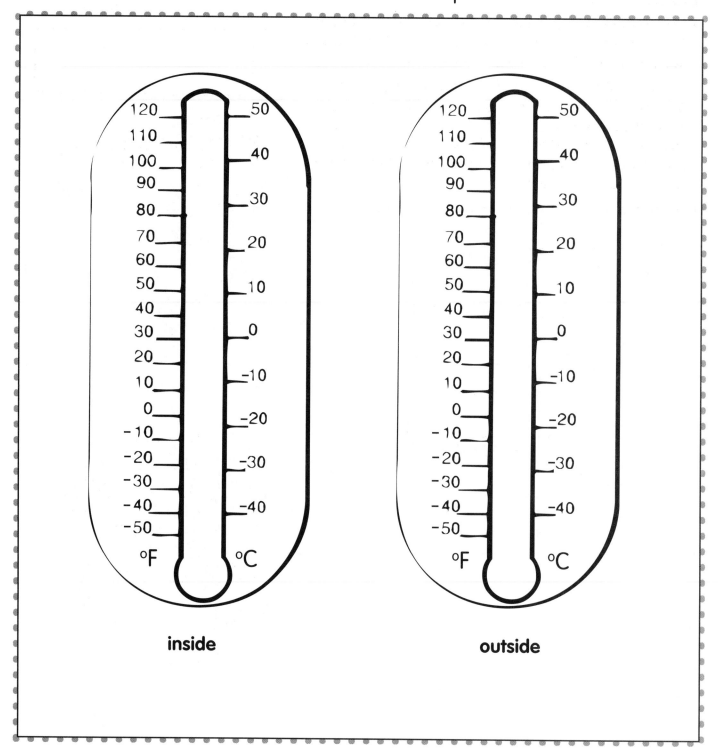

inside

outside

Making Wind

- Guide students through these steps to make paper fans. Have students use the fans to create wind. Ask, "How did you make wind?" *(pushed air/made the air move)*

- Read *Can You See the Wind?* by Allan Fowler and/or *Feel the Wind* by Arthur Dorros. Ask, "How do we know air is around us when we can't see it?" *(We can see things move in the wind. We can feel it on our face and in our hair.)* Have students enact being a gentle breeze blowing and then a strong wind.

- Write student responses about wind on a chart.

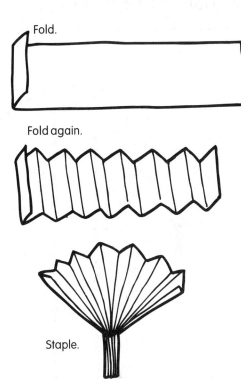

Fold.

Fold again.

Staple.

Wind

I can feel the wind.

Wind moves things.

I can feel the wind.

Learning for Myself—Measuring Wind

Explain to students that they are going to measure the wind two different ways.

Part 1
We Can Measure Wind Direction

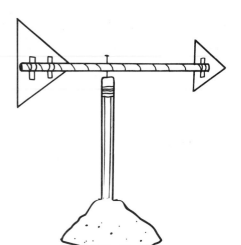

Materials

- wind vane (see construction diagram on page 4)
- masking tape
- chalk
- record sheet on page 56, reproduced for each student

Steps to Follow

1. Tape a large square on the playground. Mark *north*, *south*, *east*, and *west* with chalk. Place the wind vane in the center of the square. Explain that the arrow will point to the direction the wind is coming from.

2. Check the weather vane three times during the day. Have students stand on the same side of the wind vane during each observation as they watch to see which way the wind is blowing. Make a chalk arrow on the ground to record the wind's direction.

   At each observation, have students draw an arrow on their record sheets showing the wind direction. After the third observation, check the chalk marks to see how the wind changed direction throughout the day.

3. Have students describe how they measured wind direction. Add this to the chart "We Can Measure Weather" (page 48).

4. Place completed record sheets in students' logbooks.

page 56

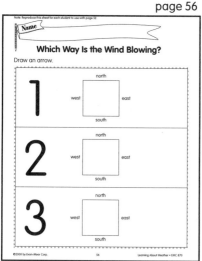

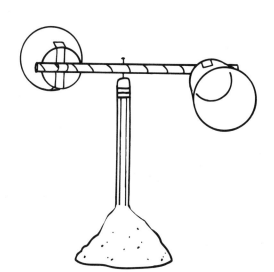

Students will observe changes in wind speed in general terms such as "fast," "slow," or "no wind."

Materials

- anemometer (see construction diagram on page 4)

- record sheet on page 57, reproduced for each student

Steps to Follow

1. Place the wind gauge outside. Check the wind speed three times during the day. Observe it to see how fast the wind is moving. Ask students to decide if the wind is moving fast, slow, or not at all.

   At each observation, have students record what they see on their record sheets.

2. At the end of the day, discuss the changes in wind speed they observed. Ask students to think of times when it is important to know how fast the wind is blowing.

3. Have students describe how they measured wind speed. Add this to the "We Can Measure Weather" chart (page 48).

4. Place completed record sheets in the students' logbooks.

page 57

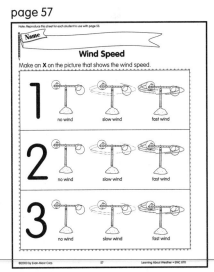

Making Connections—Wind Does Work

- Explain that because it is moving, wind can do work. Ask students to think of a way wind does this. Use questioning to help them express their ideas. Ask,

> "How does wind help a sailboat move?"
>
> "How can the wind help plant seeds move from one place to another?"
>
> "Can you think of a toy that needs the wind to move?" *(kite, pinwheel, toy sailboat, whistle)*
>
> "How does the wind make each toy move?"

Wind is moving my boat.

- Bring in an assortment of toys (e.g., pinwheel, sailboat, whistle, kite, drum, car). Have students sort the toys into two sets—those that need moving air (wind) to work and those that do not.

- Work with students to complete a chart about how wind does work.

- Have students make pinwheels to observe wind at work.

Make a Pinwheel

Materials

- pattern on page 58, reproduced for each student
- crayons
- paper fastener
- plastic drinking straw
- hole punch

Steps to Follow

1. Decorate the pinwheel with patterns or symbols representing weather (clouds, suns, rainbows, raindrops, etc.).

2. Cut out the pinwheel.

3. Punch holes in the pinwheel and straw. (This may require adult assistance.)

4. Put the pinwheel together as shown, using the paper fastener.

Using the Pinwheel

Have students try to figure out two ways to get the pinwheels to work. Have them try the methods they suggest to see what works best. Take the pinwheels outside and observe the wind doing its job.

Have students complete pages 59 and 60 to review the concept that wind can do work.

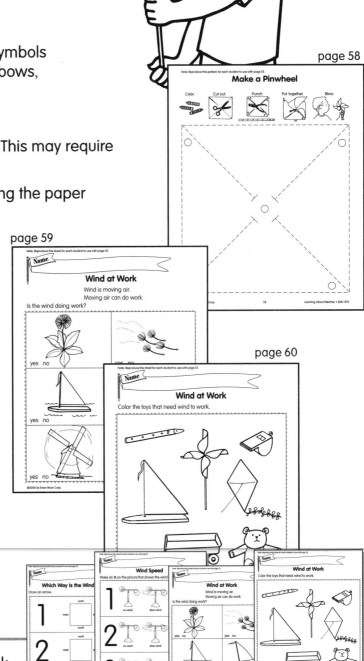

Include these pages in each student's logbook.

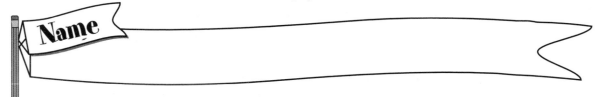

Name

Which Way Is the Wind Blowing?

Draw an arrow.

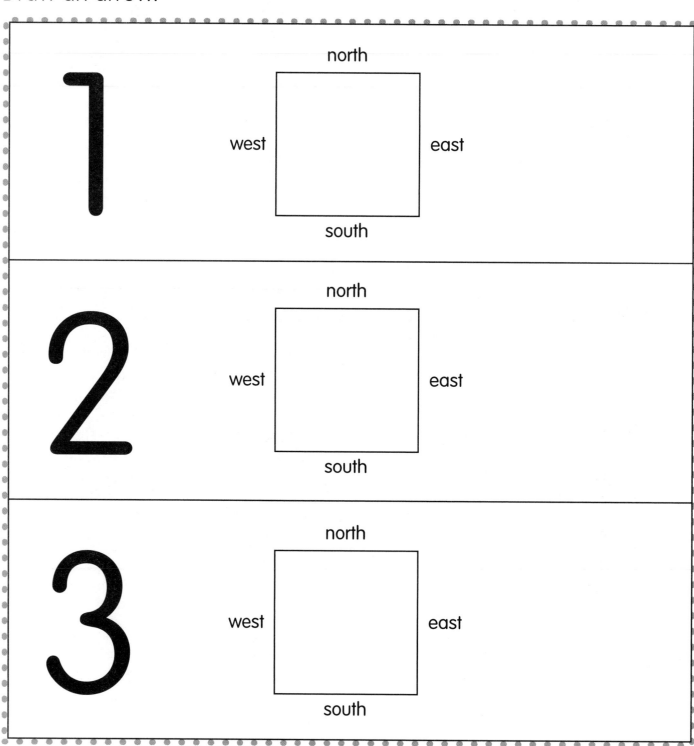

1

north

west

east

south

2

north

west

east

south

3

north

west

east

south

Name

Wind Speed

Make an **X** on the picture that shows the wind speed.

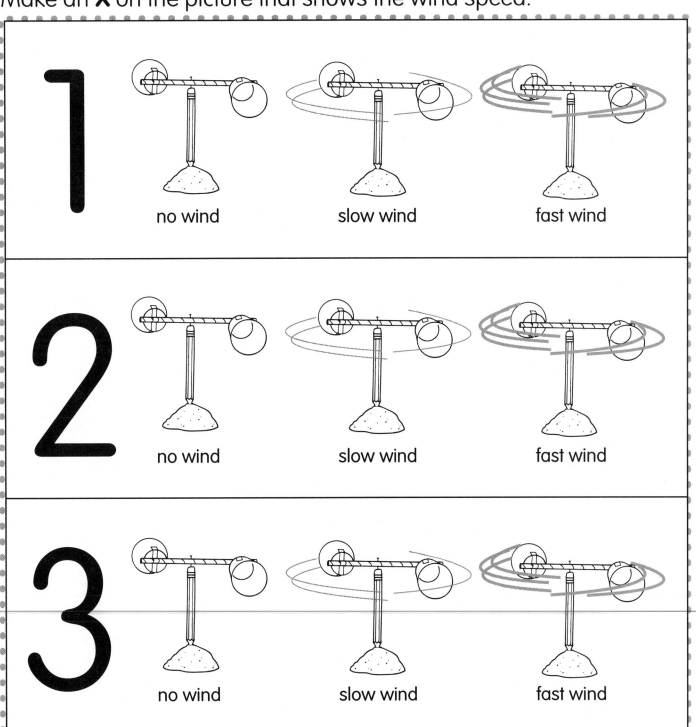

Make a Pinwheel

Color.	Cut out.	Punch.	Put together.	Blow.

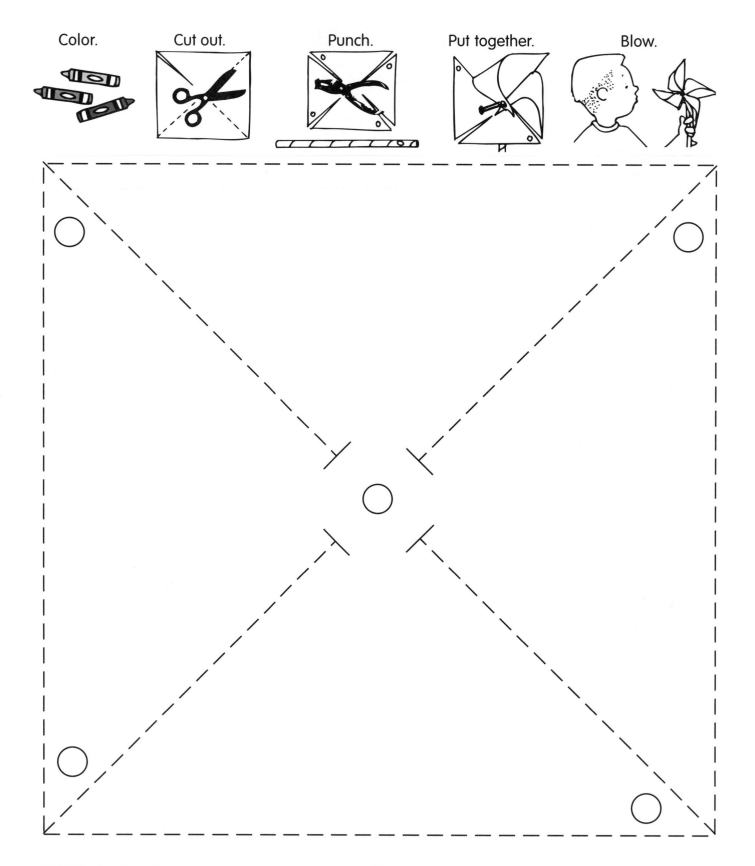

Name

Wind at Work

Wind is moving air.

Moving air can do work.

Is the wind doing work?

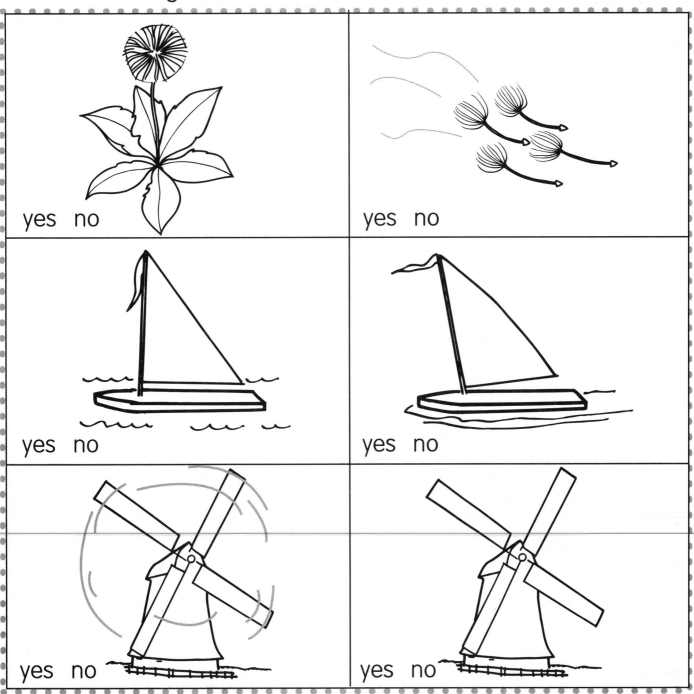

yes   no

yes   no

yes   no

yes   no

yes   no

yes   no

Learning About Weather • EMC 870

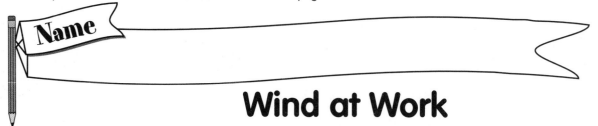

Name

Wind at Work

Color the toys that need wind to work.

Materials can exist in different states.

Liquids

Show a glass of water and a glass of juice. Ask students to name and describe what they see. Explain that things like water and juice are called *liquids*. Have students name other liquids.

List the liquids named by students on a chart. Make a small sketch of the item to help students read the list.

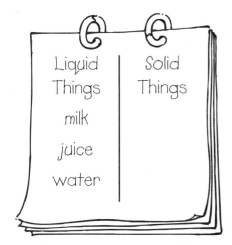

Solids

Follow the same procedure used with liquids to introduce *solids*. List solid items found in the classroom.

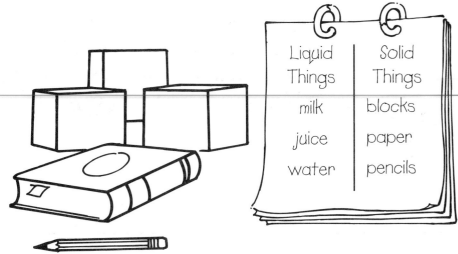

Liquid or Solid?

- Provide an assortment of liquids in closed containers and solid objects. Have students sort them into sets. Ask students to explain how they decide which item goes into each set.

  Have students think of other things that are solid or liquid. Add these to the chart.

- Show a glass of water and an ice cube. Explain that both of these are forms of water. Have students describe the differences between them.

- Students categorize solids and liquids, using pages 64 and 65.

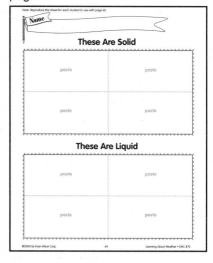

page 64

page 65

Gases

Note: *If you feel your students are ready for a more difficult concept, introduce the word* gas, *following the steps below.*

- Bring out an empty box with a lid on it. Have students guess what's inside the box. Open the lid and ask students to describe what is in the box. If the students don't guess the correct answer, tell them that the box is full of air. Spend a few moments discussing what they know about air.

- Ask students to think of things they know that contain air *(balls, balloons)*. Do the following demonstration to prove that seemingly empty containers hold air.

Observing a Gas

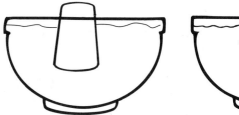

Materials

- clear glass bowl
- clear plastic drinking glass
- water
- food coloring

Steps to Follow

1. Fill the bowl with water. Add a few drops of food coloring to make it easier to observe the air in the glass.

2. Hold the "empty" glass upside down and press it down into the water. Make sure it is straight up and down. Look at the glass through the water. Ask, "Why doesn't the water go into the glass?" Provide the answer if no one responds ("Air in the glass keeps the water out").

3. Tip the glass just a little so that a bubble of air can escape. (This allows some water to go into the glass.) Tip the glass until all the air is gone. (The glass should now be filled with water.)

4. Have students describe what they observed. *(I saw bubbles in the water. There was air in the glass.)*

   Encourage them to relate what they saw to the idea that air is all around us.

page 66

- Using page 66, students color the items that are filled with air.

- Extend students' understanding by reading the appropriate parts of *What Is the World Made of?: All About Solids, Liquids, and Gases* by Kathleen Weidner Zoehfeld.

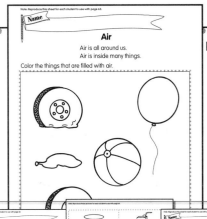

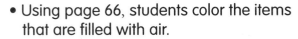

Include these pages in each student's logbook.

Note: Reproduce this sheet for each student to use with page 62.

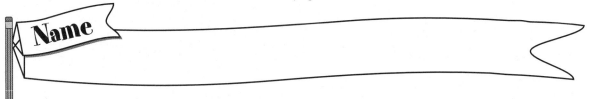

Name

These Are Solid

paste	paste
paste	paste

These Are Liquid

paste	paste
paste	paste

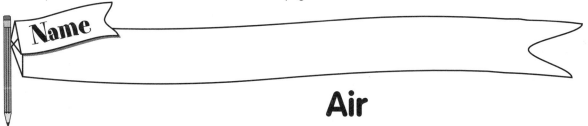

Name

Air

Air is all around us.
Air is inside many things.

Color the things that are filled with air.

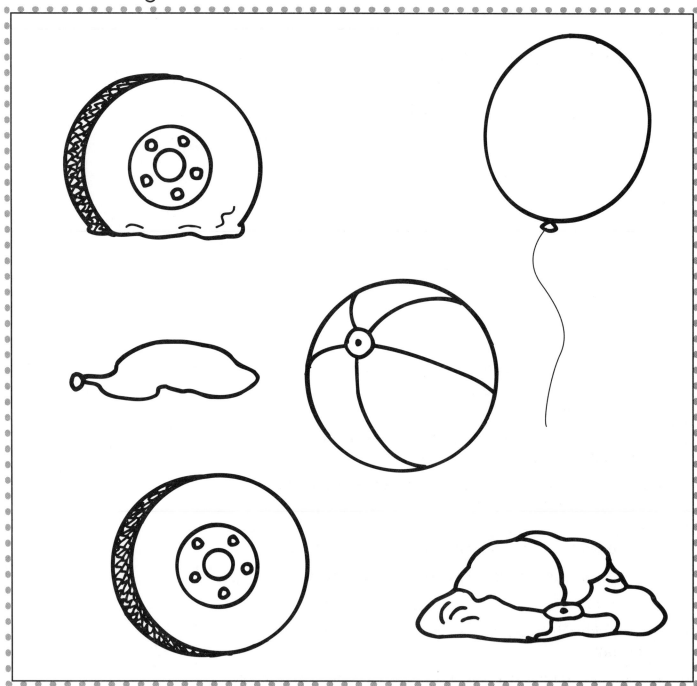

Water can change from one form to another.

Learning for Myself—Forms of Water

Say, "One of the liquids we have talked about is water. Where have you seen water around our school? Where have you seen water at home?" Explain to students that water isn't always a liquid. It can change forms.

Do the following three investigations to observe how water changes form. After each investigation,

• place completed record sheets in students' logbooks, and
• add a description of what happened to a chart entitled "Cold and Heat Change Water."

Cold Changes Water

Materials (for each group)

• water
• 2 plastic drinking glasses
• record sheet on page 70, reproduced for each student
• permanent marking pen
• access to a freezer

Steps to Follow

1. Students write their names on their glasses, fill them two-thirds full, then draw a line to mark the water level.

2. Place one glass in the freezer and leave one on a table in the classroom. Leave the glasses in each location for several hours.

3. Record student predictions on the chalkboard about what will happen to the water in each location.

4. Groups retrieve their glasses, complete their record sheets, and share what they've discovered. Ask,

page 70

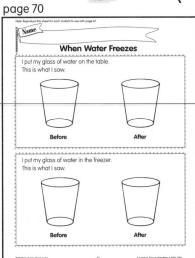

"What kind of change did you see?" *(The water in the freezer changed to ice. The water in the room didn't change.)*

"What word do we use when water changes to ice?" *(freezing)*

"The water was a liquid. What do we call it now?" *(ice; solid)*

"Why didn't the water on the table freeze?" *(It wasn't cold enough.)*

5. Compare group results with the predictions on the chalkboard.

Heat Changes Water

Now ask students to tell you what they think happens when ice gets warm. Conduct the following investigations to check their answers.

Materials (for each student)

- small plastic cup
- ice cube
- paper towels
- permanent marking pen
- page 71, reproduced for each student

Steps to Follow

1. Students write their name on their cup, place an ice cube in it, and set it in sunlight.

2. Ask students to predict what will happen.

3. Have students observe their ice cubes periodically. Ask,

   "What change do you see?" *(The ice cube is melting.)*
   "What is it now—a solid or a liquid?"

4. When the ice cubes have melted completely, have students complete their record sheets. Then ask them to explain what caused the ice to melt. If necessary, use questioning to help them articulate that ice must be kept cold. When it gets warm, the ice melts, turning back into a liquid. Compare the results with their predictions.

page 71

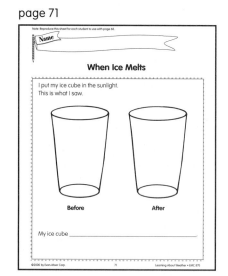

Water Becomes a Gas

Materials (for each group)

- water
- jar with a lid
- jar without a lid
- measuring cup
- black marking pen
- record sheet on page 72, reproduced for each student

Steps to Follow

1. Students put the same amount of water in a jar with a lid and an open jar. They place both jars on a windowsill and leave the jars overnight.

2. Ask students to predict what will happen to the water in each jar.

3. Observe the water level in each jar the next morning. Ask students to think about what happened to the water in the open jar. Help them understand that the missing water went up into the air. Ask why the water in the closed jar didn't go into the air. *(The lid kept it in.)*

   Help students complete their record sheets.

Making Connections

- Make an overhead transparency of page 73. Also reproduce a copy for each student. Show the transparency. Have students find water everywhere it exists in the picture, and then color the water on their copies.

- Reproduce the water drop booklet on pages 74–77 for each student. They are to cut out and staple the booklet together, and take it home to share with parents.

page 72

page 73

Include these pages in each student's logbook.

Learning About Weather • EMC 870

Note: Reproduce this sheet for each student to use with page 67.

Name

When Water Freezes

I put my glass of water on the table.
This is what I saw.

Before

After

I put my glass of water in the freezer.
This is what I saw.

Before

After

Note: Reproduce this sheet for each student to use with page 68.

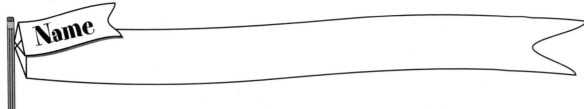

Name

When Ice Melts

I put my ice cube in the sunlight.
This is what I saw.

Before

After

My ice cube _____.

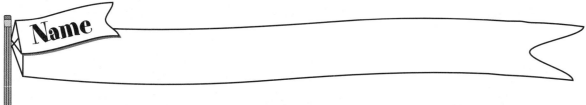

Name

Where Did the Water Go?

Color the water in each jar.

Before

After

The water went _____.

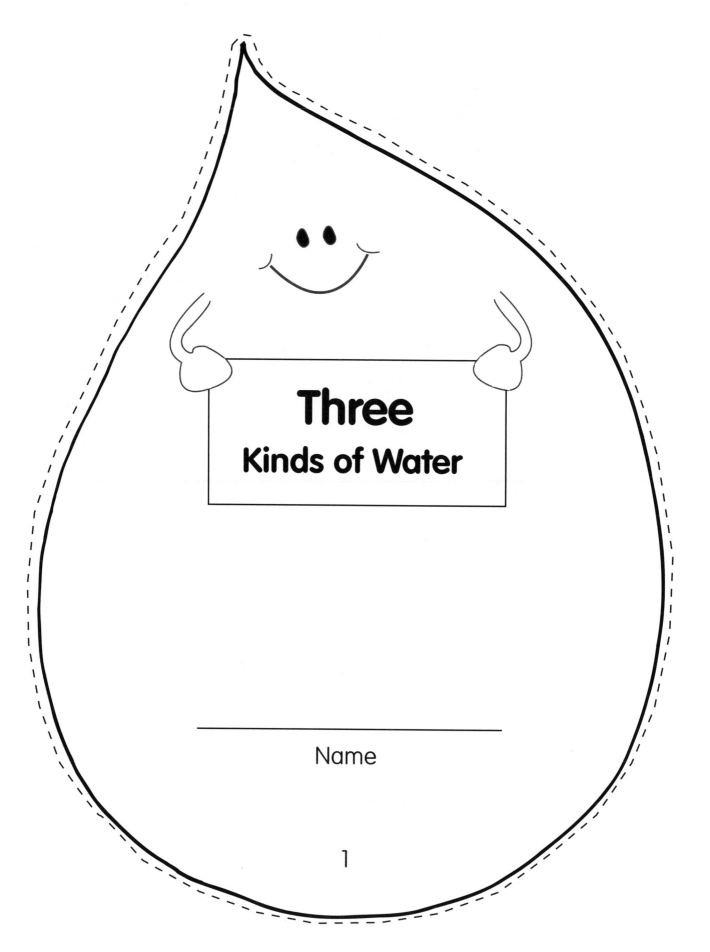

Three
Kinds of Water

_____

Name

1

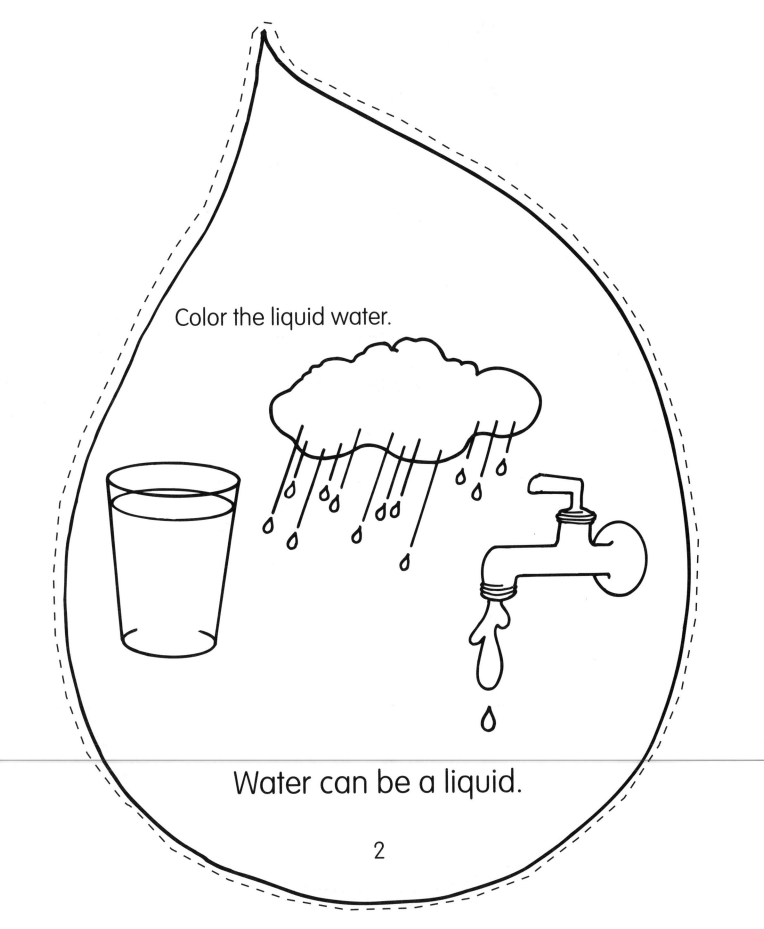

Color the liquid water.

Water can be a liquid.

2

Learning About Weather • EMC 870

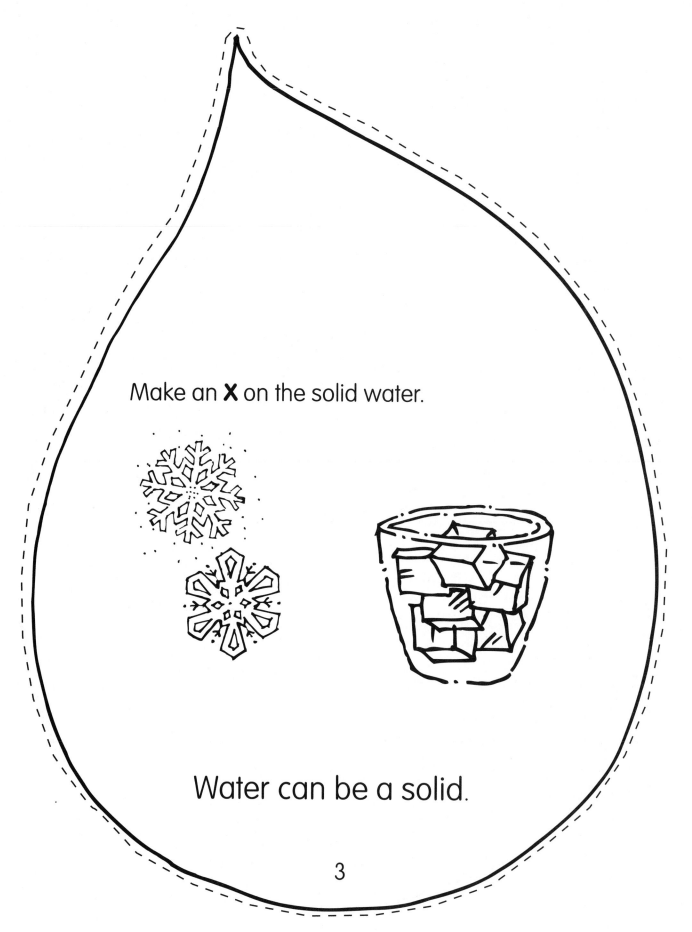

Make an **X** on the solid water.

Water can be a solid.

3

Learning About Weather • EMC 870

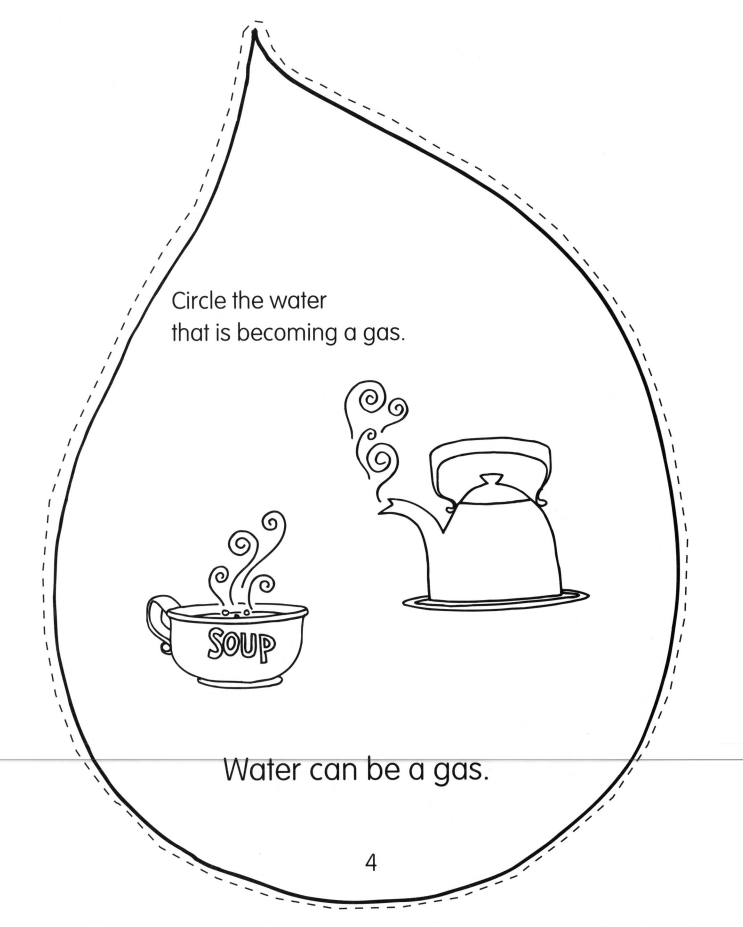

Circle the water
that is becoming a gas.

Water can be a gas.

4

Learning About Weather • EMC 870

Rain is part of the water cycle.

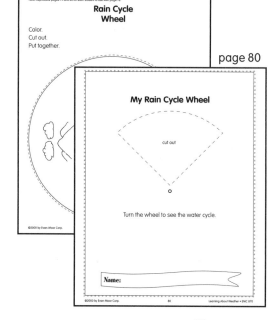

The Water Cycle

- Explain that some things in nature happen over and over again. This repetition is called a *cycle*. Recall what students learned about the cycle of the seasons (Spring, summer, autumn, and winter occur in the same order each year). Ask students to name other things that happen in a cycle (e.g., days of the week, growth of a plant).

- Use the rain cycle wheel on pages 79 and 80 to introduce the water cycle.

  Note: *Do not expect students to completely understand the process at this age. It is enough that they know that water can change form, go up into the air, and then come down as rain. You are setting the groundwork for greater understanding in later grades.*

  Each student will need a brass paper fastener to connect the wheel to its folder. Have students share what they see as they turn the completed wheel.

- Read *Down Comes the Rain* by Franklyn M. Branley or appropriate parts of *Water, Water Everywhere: A Book About the Water Cycle* by Melvin Berger and Gilda Berger to reinforce learning about the water cycle.

- Have students recall what they have learned about rain and the water cycle. Make changes and add information to the "Rain" chart begun on page 7.

page 79

page 80

Making Connections

Discuss how rain can be fun (walking in the rain with boots and an umbrella; seeing rainbows; splashing in puddles) and how it can be a problem (have to stay indoors; too much rain causes floods).

drip

splash

plop

Rain

Drops of water fall out of the sky.

Rain comes from clouds.

Learning About Weather • EMC 870

Rain Cycle
Wheel

Color.
Cut out.
Put together.

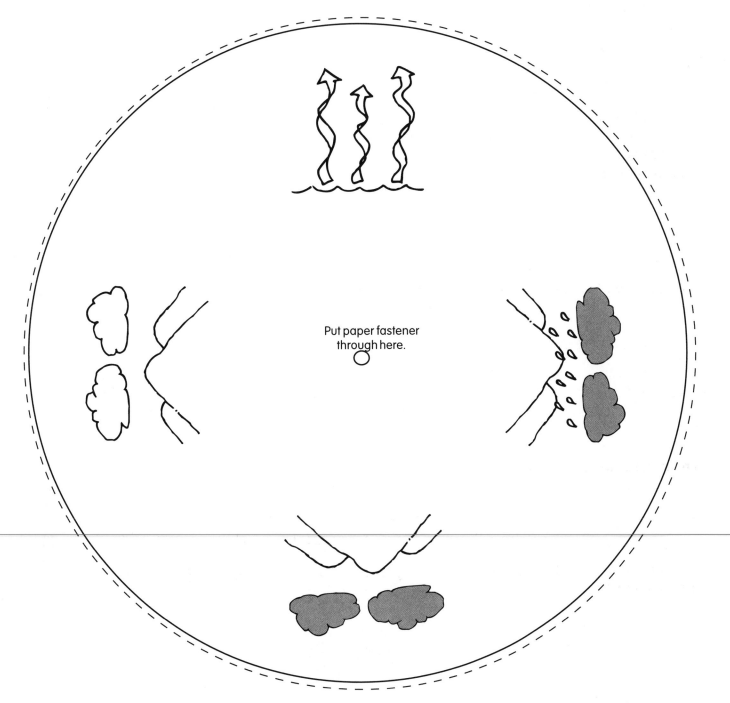

Put paper fastener
through here.

My Rain Cycle Wheel

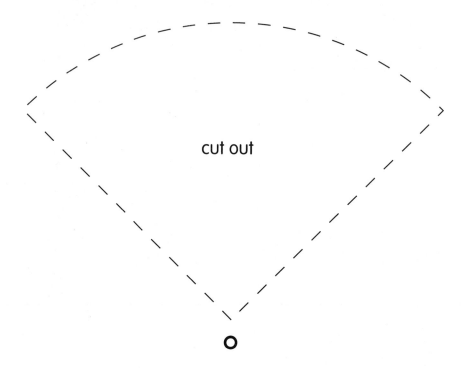

cut out

Turn the wheel to see the water cycle.

Name: